WHAT A KINGDOM IT WAS

BY GALWAY KINNELL

WHAT A KINGDOM IT WAS

HOUGHTON MIFFLIN COMPANY BOSTON

THE RIVERSIDE PRESS CAMBRIDGE · 1960

Certain of the poems in this volume have previously appeared in various books
and magazines as follows:

The *Atlantic Monthly*: "Freedom, New Hampshire." Copyright © 1960 by
The Atlantic Monthly Company.

The *Beloit Poetry Journal*: "Westport." Copyright 1953 by *The Beloit Poetry
Journal*. Also "First Communion" and "First Song."

Epoch: "Easter." Copyright 1953 by Epoch Associates.

The Hudson Review: "The Avenue Bearing the Initial of Christ into the New
World." Copyright 1960 by The Hudson Review, Inc.

Modern Age: A somewhat different version of "Leaping Falls" under the title
"Spicatto". Copyright © 1957 by the Foundation for Foreign Affairs, Inc.
"The Schoolhouse." Copyright © by the Foundation for Foreign Affairs, Inc.

The Nation: "Earth-Sparrow," "In a Parlor Containing a Table," "At the
Reading of a Poet's Will." Copyright 1958, 1959, 1960 by the Nation
Associates, Inc.

The New Orleans Poetry Journal: "One Generation."

New Poems by American Poets — Volume I: "For the Lost Generation," "For
William Carlos Williams." Copyright 1953 by Ballantine Books, Inc. "First
Song." Copyright 1953 by Galway Kinnell. Volume II: "Near Barbizon,"
"Leaping Falls." © 1957 by Ballantine Books, Inc.

New World Writing #3: "First Song." Copyright 1953 by The New American Library of World Literature, Inc.

The New Yorker: "Reply to the Provinces." © 1958 by The New Yorker
Magazine, Inc.

Noonday II: "Duck-Chasing." Copyright © 1959 by The Noonday Press, Inc.

Perspective: "A Toast to Tu Fu," "Burning." Copyright 1954 by *Perspective*.

The Pocket Book of Modern Verse: "To Christ Our Lord." © 1954 Pocket
Books, Inc.

Poetry: "The Wolves," "Across the Brown River," "Lilacs," "Alewives Pool,"
"Seven Streams of Nevis," "The Descent," "Where the Track Vanishes,"
"For Ruth." Copyright 1953, 1955, 1957, 1958, 1959, 1960 by Modern
Poetry Association.

The Prairie Schooner: "Rain over a Continent." Copyright 1958 by the Uni-
versity of Nebraska Press.

Voices: "Gothic Slide." Copyright 1954 by Harold Vinal.

TO CHARLES AND DIANA BELL

CONTENTS

PART III

PART IV

PART I

FIRST SONG

Then it was dusk in Illinois, the small boy
After an afternoon of carting dung
Hung on the rail fence, a sapped thing
Weary to crying. Dark was growing tall
And he began to hear the pond frogs all
Calling on his ear with what seemed their joy.

Soon their sound was pleasant for a boy
Listening in the smoky dusk and the nightfall
Of Illinois, and from the fields two small
Boys came bearing cornstalk violins
And they rubbed the cornstalk bows with resins
And the three sat there scraping of their joy.

It was now fine music the frogs and the boys
Did in the towering Illinois twilight make
And into dark in spite of a shoulder's ache
A boy's hunched body loved out of a stalk
The first song of his happiness, and the song woke
His heart to the darkness and into the sadness of joy.

FIRST COMMUNION

The church is way over in the next county,
The same trip that last year we trekked
Carrying a sackful of ears to collect
The nickel-an-ear porcupine bounty.
Pictured on the wall over dark Jerusalem
Jesus is shining — in the dark he is a lamp.
On the tray he is a pastry wafer.
On the way home, there is regular talk
Of the fine preaching, before the regular jokes
Are allowed. The last time over
The same trail we brought two dollars homeward.
Now we carry the aftertaste of the Lord.
Soon a funny story about Uncle Abraham:
How, being liquored up, he got locked out
By his woman; how she must have taken blankets out
Later, for Sam says he found them, in the morning,
Asleep in each other's arms in the loft.

The sunlight streams through the afternoon
Another parable over the sloughs
And yellowing grass of the prairies.
Cold wind stirs, and the last green
Climbs to all the tips of the season, like
The last flame brightening on a wick.
Embers drop and break in sparks. Across the earth
Sleep is the overlapping of enough shadows.
In the wind outside a twig snaps
Like a lid shutting somewhere in the ear.
Jesus, a boy thinks as his room goes out,

Jesus, it is a disappointing shed
Where they hang your picture
And drink juice, and conjure
Your person into inferior bread —
I would speak of injustice . . .
I would not go again into that place . . .

TO CHRIST OUR LORD

The legs of the elk punctured the snow's crust
And wolves floated lightfooted on the land
Hunting Christmas elk living and frozen;
Inside snow melted in a basin, and a woman basted
A bird spread over coals by its wings and head.

Snow had sealed the windows; candles lit
The Christmas meal. The Christmas grace chilled
The cooked bird, being long-winded and the room cold.
During the words a boy thought, is it fitting
To eat this creature killed on the wing?

He had killed it himself, climbing out
Alone on snowshoes in the Christmas dawn,
The fallen snow swirling and the snowfall gone,
Heard its throat scream as the rifle shouted,
Watched it drop, and fished from the snow the dead.

He had not wanted to shoot. The sound
Of wings beating into the hushed air
Had stirred his love, and his fingers
Froze in his gloves, and he wondered,
Famishing, could he fire? Then he fired.

Now the grace praised his wicked act. At its end
The bird on the plate
Stared at his stricken appetite.
There had been nothing to do but surrender,
To kill and to eat; he ate as he had killed, with wonder.

At night on snowshoes on the drifting field
He wondered again, for whom had love stirred?
The stars glittered on the snow and nothing answered.
Then the Swan spread her wings, cross of the cold north,
The pattern and mirror of the acts of earth.

BURNING

He lives, who last night flopped from a log
Into the creek, and all night by an ankle
Lay pinned to the flood, dead as a nail
But for the skin of the teeth of his dog.

I brought him boiled eggs and broth.
He coughed and waved his spoon
And sat up saying he would dine alone,
Being fatigue itself after that bath.

I sat without in the sun with the dog.
Wearing a stocking on the ailing foot,
In monster crutches, he hobbled out,
And addressed the dog in bitter rage.

He told the yellow hound, his rescuer,
Its heart was bad, and it ought
Not wander by the creek at night;
If all his dogs got drowned he would be poor.

He stroked its head and disappeared in the shed
And came out with a stone mallet in his hands
And lifted that rocky weight of many pounds
And let it lapse on top of the dog's head.

I carted off the carcass, dug it deep.
Then he came too with what a thing to lug,
Or pour on a dog's grave, his thundermug,
And poured it out and went indoors to sleep.

I saw him sleepless in the pane of glass
Looking wild-eyed at sunset, then the glare
Blinded the glass — only a red square
Burning a house burning in the wilderness.

THE WOLVES

Last night knives flashed. LeChien cried
And chewed blood in his bed.
Vanni's whittling blade
Had found flesh easier than wood.

Vanni and I left camp on foot. In a glade
We came on a brown blossom
Great and shining on a thorned stem.
"That's the sensitive briar," I said.

"It shrinks at the touch," I added.
Soon we found buffalo. Picking
A bull grazing by itself, I began
The approach: while the shaggy head

Was turned I sprinted across the sod,
And when he swung around his gaze
I bellyflopped in the grass
And lay on my heartbeat and waited.

When he looked away again I made
Enough yardage before he wheeled
His head: I kneeled, levelled
My rifle, and we calmly waited.

It occurred to me as we waited
That in those last moments he was,
In fact, daydreaming about something else.
"He is too stupid to live," I said.

His legs shifted and the heart showed.
I fired. He looked, trotted off,
He simply looked and trotted off,
Stumbled, sat himself down, and became dead.

I looked for Vanni. Amid the cows he stood,
Only his arms moving as he fired,
Loaded, and fired, the dumb herd
Milling about him sniffing at their dead.

I called and he retreated.
We cut two choice tongues for ourselves
And left the surplus. All day wolves
Would splash blood from those great sides.

Again we saw the flower, brown-red
On a thorn-spiked stem. When Vanni
Extended his fingers, it was funny,
It shrank away as if it had just died.

They told us in camp that LeChien was dead.
None of us cared. Nobody much
Had liked him. His tobacco pouch,
I observed, was already missing from beside his bed.

WESTPORT

From the hilltop we could overlook
The changes on the world. Behind us
Spread the forest, that half a continent away
Had met our fathers on the Atlantic shore.
Before us lay a narrow belt of brush.
And everywhere beyond, shifting like an ocean,
Swell upon swell of emerald green,
The prairies of the west were blowing.

We mounted and set out, small craft
Into the green. The grasses brushed
The bellies of the horses, and under
The hooves the knotted centuries of sod
Slowed the way. Here and there the grey
Back of a wolf breached and fell, as in the grass
Their awkward voyages appeared and vanished.

Then rain lashed down in a savage squall.
All afternoon it drove us west. "It will be
A long, hard journey," the boy said, "and look,
We are blown like the weed." And indeed we were . . .
O wild indigo, O love-lies-bleeding,
You, prince's feather, pigweed, and bugseed,
Hold your ground as you can. We toss ahead
Of you in the wild rain, and we barely touch
The sad ambages compassed for yourselves.

When the storm abated, a red streak in the west
Lit all the raindrops on the land before us.
"Yes," I said, "it will be a hard journey . . ."

And the shining grasses were bowed towards the west
As if one craving had killed them. "But at last,"
I added, "the hardness is the thing you thank."
So out of forest we sailed onto plains,
And from the dark afternoon came a bright evening.

Now out of evening we discovered night
And heard the cries of the prairie and the moan
Of wind through the roots of its clinging flowers.

PART II

AT THE READING OF A POET'S WILL

Item. A desk
Smelling of ink and turpentine
To anyone whose task
Is to sweat rain for a line.

Item. A sheaf
Of poems, a few lucid,
One or two brief,
To anyone who will bid.

*   *   *

Item. Praise Jesus, who spent
His last cent
In the wild woods of himself in the try
For self-mastery.

His boast
Is that though he did insist
On principle, in terror and compromise
He taught us what love's limit is.

Item. I built a desk,
I spent myself for a sheaf,
All else I committed I ask
That the Lord forgive.

I took Christ for my pattern,
Once he was kind to a slattern,
If I was led into mazes
Blame and praise Jesus. *Amen.*

LILACS

The wind climbed with a laggard pace
Up the green hill, and meeting the sun there
Disappeared like a piece of warm wax
Into the ground. Down on the south slope
A bitch stretched, and swaths of fierce lilacs
Opened astonishing furnaces of scent.

A woman introduced herself into the park,
Her dry legs crackling in darkness
At bitch, lilac, the fierce and asleep.
Summer slopped like a flood at her knees,
The hot scent of herself beating herself
Out of closets in the well-governed flesh.

She stopped. The blossoms climbed
And blazed in the air, and the lawn slowly
Somersaulted under her. She turned back
To the narrow parlor, where tea and dry supper
Would be laid, and a spoon would arrange
The leaves on the bottom of her china dream.

A TOAST TO TU FU

To you, Tu Fu,
Because it didn't work out
When you lent
Yourself to government.
A poet isn't made to fix
Things up — only to celebrate
What's down, and in politics
As that Irishman found out
Is a lout.

To you, Tu Fu,
For fooling the crew
Who thought trial
Must make a man good;
And for, when the waters rose
Around the temple
You clung to in the flood,
While they prayed you'd
Let go with a prayer,
Having hung on like a bear.

And again to you, Tu Fu,
For gorging at the feast
Honoring your rescue,
For not mentioning virtue
In your short speech, nor praising rot,
And for having had the appetite and timing
To die of overeating on the spot.

EASTER

We read of her death in the morning.
By the riverbank shreds of clothes and her purse.
Raped, robbed, weighted, drowned —
They conjecture the night-off of a virgin nurse.

To get to church you have to cross the river,
First breadwinner for the town, its wide
Mud-colored currents cleansing forever
The swill-making villages at its side.

The disinfected voice of the minister
For a moment is one of the clues,
But he is talking of nothing but Easter,
Dying so on the wood, He rose.

Some of us daydream of the morning news,
Some of us lament we rose at all,
A child beside me comforts her doll,
We are dying on the hard wood of the pews.

Death is everywhere, in the extensive
Sermon, the outcry of the inaudible
Prayer, the nickels, the dimes the poor give,
And outside, at last, in the gusts of April.

Upon the river, its Walden calm,
With wire hooks the little boats are fishing.
Those who can wait to get home
Line up, and lean on the railing, wishing.

Up through the mud can you see us
Waiting here for you, for hours,
Virgin lady, trapped or working loose,
Can you see our hats like a row of flowers?

Then we crown you with an Easter fire,
And if you do not rise before dinner
When the flower show must bow and retire,
Then drink well of the breadwinner,

And tomorrow when the brown water
Shall shove you senselessly on
Past smoking cities, works of disaster,
Kids playing ball, cows, unrealistic fishermen,

Toll bridges you slip under for free,
And you cast an eye from the brown lorry
Which floats your drenching flesh to sea,
Do not, moved by goodbyes, be altogether sorry

That the dream has ended. Turn
On the dream you lived through the unwavering gaze.
It is as you thought. The living burn.
In the floating days may you discover grace.

FOR WILLIAM CARLOS WILLIAMS

When you came and you talked and you read with your
Private zest from the varicose marble
Of the podium, the lovers of literature
Paid you the tribute of their almost total
Inattention, although someone when you spoke of a pig
Did squirm, and it is only fair to report another gig-

gled. But you didn't even care. You seemed
Above remarking we were not your friends.
You hung around inside the rimmed
Circles of your heavy glasses and smiled and
So passed a lonely evening. In an hour
Of talking your honesty built you a tower.

When it was over and you sat down and the chair-
man got up and smiled and congratulated
You and shook your hand, I watched a professor
In neat bow tie and enormous tweeds, who patted
A faint praise of the sufficiently damned,
Drained spittle from his pipe, then scrammed.

FOR THE LOST GENERATION

Oddities composed the sum of the news.
$E = mc^2$
Was another weird
Sign of the existence of the Jews.

And Paris! All afternoon in someone's attic
We lifted our glasses
And drank to the asses
Who ran the world and turned neurotic.

Ours was a wonderful party,
Everyone threw rice,
The fattest girls were nice,
The world was rich in wisecracks and confetti.

The War was a first wife, somebody's blunder.
Who was right, who lost,
Held nobody's interest,
The dog on top was as bad as the dog under.

Sometimes after whiskey, at the break of day,
There was a trace
Of puzzlement on a face,
Face of blue nights that kept bleaching away.

Look back on it all — the faraway cost,
Crash and sweet blues
(O Hiroshima, O Jews) —
No generation was so gay as the lost.

ALEWIVES POOL

1

We lay on the grass and gazed down and heard
The world burning on the pulse of April,
And were so shaken and stirred, so cut, we wondered
Which things may we forget and which recall?
We rose to find out and we flew like birds

And flew down the path to the Alewives Pool
Where herring driven by lust from the seas
Came flocking up until the pond would spill;
And fell amazed — how they memorize
Love's never-studied maps and ritual.

2

A dying lady from her bed once told
The row of faces dimming in her glance,
Who came to her party at four years old,
What frills each wore, who laughed, who could not dance,
Who cried, whose hand she did not let hers hold.

The infant searches at his mother's breast
Looking for the night he was shipwrecked from —
But when he finds her milk he suddenly tastes
A brightness that scares him, and his days to come
Flood on his heart as if they were his past.

3

Grass lies as though beating under the wind.
In the trees even the birds are astonished
By the fierce passion of their song. The mind
Can only know what love has accomplished
When love has consumed it in the burning pond.

Now on the trembling pulse let death and birth
Beat in the self as in the April grass —
The sudden summer that the air flames forth
Makes us again into its blossomers —
Stand on the pulse and love the burning earth.

LEAPING FALLS

And so it was I sheered,
Eccentric, into outer space,
And tracked with lost paces
The forgotten journey of a child,
Across the creaking snow,
Up the deer-trail,

Over the snowdrifted hill
Into the secret country
Where a boy once found,
Routing from ledge to ledge
In a tumult at sunrise,
The downrush of Leaping Falls.

Now they were draped
Without motion or sound,
Icicles fastened in stories
To stillness and rock. Underneath,
A heap of icicles, broken,
Lay dead blue on the snow.

Cold was through and through,
Noiseless. Nothing
Except clouds at my nostrils
Moved. Then I uttered a word,
Simply a bleak word
Slid from the lips. Whereupon

A topmost icicle came loose
And fell, and struck another
With a bell-like sound, and
Another, and the falls
Leapt at their ledges, ringing
Down the rocks and on each other

Like an outbreak of bells
That rings and ceases.
The silence turned around
And became silence again.
Under the falls on the snow
A twigfire of icicles burned pale blue.

PROMONTORY MOON

The moon: she shakes off her cloaks,
Her rings of mist and circle of blurred light,
And shines without chemistry or heat
Upon us. Milky blue in her influence
The sea rises dabbing at the tiers of rock.
A few shadowy rabbits dash feinting
Over the grass and paths. In sunlight
Men will sprawl generating on the grass;
But the rabbits ask nothing of the moon,
And run at midnight for delight alone.

Half rabbits, half rabbits' shadows,
They are like the night-roistering fairies
For whom as children we set banquets
In the dusk, of bits of bread and honey,
That we explored for in the dawn and found
Untouched, the one trace of fairies being
The dew glistening on the moss and grass
At daybreak, which they shed for sorrow
Their weightless bodies have no appetite,
Being woven by the night of moonlight.

The sun makes the grass increase, feeding
The things it can corrupt. The moon
Holds her purer watches on the night,
Mirroring on that fairest time of day
Only the subtlest miracles of light;
And that within ourselves too straight to bend

In agonies of death and birth — as now
The blue-white sea swirls at the moonbeams
And keeps on winding on the shining clew —
Dissolves at her touch and is weaved anew.

ACROSS THE BROWN RIVER

The Brown River, finger of a broken fist,
Moved sluggish through the woods and dust.
We made a bridge of the crashed oak, teetering
Across like monkeys taking up drinking,
Eschewing the deeps with our eyes,
For on the other side they said lay paradise.

It was a modern replica, built by the offspring of a rich
Dog-like dowager — some son-of-a-bitch
Who liked formal gardens of paths and shaven trees,
Hedges in a maze, and many elegant statues.
We noted "The Girl with Silk," a stone queen
With spread legs draped in the nick of time between.

In the afternoon we studied "The Last
Centaur Expiring," face folded on its breast,
All the segment that was a man pleading love
And fatal attraction for the brutal half.
A visitor beside us grew incensed
At miscegenation, and spoke out bitterly against.

We went our way at last, dancing across the oak
Into the woods. From the woods outside of Eden came a snake.
We found no principle of evil here except
Tweed packed with butter halted where it stepped,
Binoculars fixed on birds fleeing in the trees
The narrow eye, bloated in the goggles of paradise.

GOTHIC SLIDE

Above the blue wash of the lake
Where the sun is a bright spectre,
And cars run, we discourse on culture;
Then the curtains close our modern talk
And faces in the slides revive
World-famous beauty, blent of light and grief.
Who can look on the stone figures,
The fatal innocence in the stone smiles,
And not sit by the feet of desire, a credulous pupil?
Over the cloaked body and covered neck
The lips come alive, but they move alone;
How can we speak when our tongues are stone?
The curtains open and our dazed eyes wreck
On the sheer sunlight climbing like a dream
Into the darkness which had become our home.
Below, the waves return like breath
To the shores of Chicago; sunlight weaves
In flashes over the curve of the Drive
Where the cars and cares of the earth
Crawl in a line. Is it this to be human —
A flair for the ideal gone bad under the breastbone?

ONE GENERATION

Between the first and last
Of one generation, stretch vast
Reservations and grandeurs. Once in a park
Walked a girl of twenty with a gray-
haired man, her lover, a book of narrow verse
In his hand. In the sunset they sank
Down the slope together, tied by the distance
Into a knot of love, to be undone
Only by extremes and crying, and then
Never done again. An old man reading a newspaper
Sat on the hill; not far off sat a little girl.
And did their hands reach out? The night
Came over them, they fell away alone. And I
Alone on the grass: what if I now should
Touch your face, child, mother, star first and faint in the sky?

EARTH-SPARROW

The trees in clouds of November mist
Standing empty and the massive earth bare
I bent my head and leaned myself against
Interior gales and blizzards of unrest
Bucking the squalor of November air

But checked at last and skyward with shredded
Arms lifting ribbons of fingers and prayers
I caught in that beseeching of the cloud
One leafless lightning-splintered oak unshroud-
ing its wreckage in the waste of the year

To whose ultimate twig with a zoom and
Skip a sparrow summitted and there burst-
ing as if the dead sap kept singing leaned
I forward knowing nothing to lean on
Green as the grasslessness Lord of the earth.

RAIN OVER A CONTINENT

Rain over a continent, the train
From Washington to Washington plunged
In the sowing rain. He slept with
His nurse on the voyage, she was rough,
Scarred with transcontinental love,
She was his all-guessing heart when he died.
Raise the blind, he commanded. Under
The rain the continent wheeled, his own land
Electric and blind, farmlights and cities'
Blazes — points, clusters and chains —
Each light a memory and the whole of darkness
Memory. In the seedfall of a continent
The majesty of a man rendered himself home:
His death was dust on the land when he died.

REPLY TO THE PROVINCES

for Henry Braun

He writes from the provinces: it is
Shuttered and desolate there, will I please
Sit on a bench for him every so often
In the Luxembourg Gardens? So now
In the elegant autumn, to regard and guess —

The sea-eyed children watching their sloops
Angling on the flood? Expectant in their books
The delicate young women? The would-be
Casters-off of expectation? The hands-in-hands?
The fellow shucking chestnuts for his girl?
The Algerians, Americans, English, Danes
Giving the Gardens their Parisian character?
Fountained light streaming on the wind?
Surely these and things of this kind —
Whatever is human. Also I marvel at the leaves
Yellow on the sky, and there on the grass
Where the leaves overlap, yellow, the yellow sun
Forcing the hidden glowing from the earth —
I peer like an ape on a branch, on a bench —

In the provinces he may have walked from town.
In a city of leaves he may have found her. Perhaps
Already they are lying in the leaves, laughing,
Pointing out for each other the brown faces in the leaves.

NEAR BARBIZON

At first I thought some animal, wounded,
Thrashed in the brush, for the hunting horns
Had sounded last night and this morning.
No, it was only the little woodgatherer
Out after lunch for twigs for the fire.
He had his own way of breaking a branch.
Others might have laid it across two rocks
And jumped in the middle. He raised it like a flail
And beat a rock until the weapon broke.
We talked. It was election time, and I asked
Whom was he voting for. He screwed his eyes.
"If there came into your house by night
Thieves, to which would you offer your wife?"
Whacks he laid on the rock until the branch gave.
"I am too honest, merde, or too poor to vote.
There's fuel on the forest floor still."
"What's your trade?" I inquired. "Gardener."
"So you make things bloom?" "Yes, and the pay's
Nothing." He was flailing the rocks in savage, measured
Strokes. "The pay's nothing," he repeated,
Looking up without ceasing his labor, keys of both
Eyes flashing: this intellectual, this rich American, this fascist boss!

DUCK-CHASING

I spied a very small brown duck
Riding the swells of the sea
Like a rocking-chair. "Little duck!"
I cried. It paddled away,
I paddled after it. When it dived,
Down I dived: too smoky was the sea,
We were lost. It surfaced
In the west, I torpedoed west
And when it dived I dived,
And we were lost and lost and lost
In the slant smoke of the sea.
When I came floating up on it
From the side, like a deadman,
And yelled suddenly, it took off,
It skimmed the swells as it ascended,
Brown wings burning and flashing
In the sun as the sea it rose over
Burned and flashed underneath it.
I did not see the little duck again.
Duck-chasing is a game like any game.
When it is over it is all over.

FOR RUTH

It was a surprise,
Seeing you. You were
More steadfast than I remember.
On the limestone shelf
You endured yourself
With grace.

The shock was only
When you laid in on tape
Some of my speech, to escape
Into or to live through
Later on, when you would get blue —
But of course you would be lonely,

You of that fierce memory!
I saw you once remembering
A fisherman drunk as bait on a string
At the end of the bar —
Your chilled flesh went blue as a star.
A thing turns real for you eventually,

The touch is just the babytooth.
On your heap of bleached rock
You listen, wires in the mind play it back,
You hear the million sighs,
You cry for them, each simply cries
For ruth, for ruth.

IN A PARLOR CONTAINING A TABLE

In a parlor containing a table
And three chairs, three men confided
Their inmost thoughts to one another.
I, said the first, am miserable.
I am miserable, the second said.
I think that for me the correct word
Is miserable, asserted the third.
Well, they said at last, it's quarter to two.
Good night. Cheer up. Sleep well.
You too. You too. You too.

GUILLAUME DE LORRIS

His is the romance without a heroine —
Only the Rose in the Garden, far away,
Restless in shadows, longing to be plucked.
The intensity of his dream nourishing him
The hero walks the desert of this world
Towards, without swerving, l'idéale Bien-Aimée.

He comes into the Garden on broken feet
After many years: he discovers at last,
Unattended, the single, mysterious Rose.
Being old at this moment (he has walked
Half his life on the desert), he declines,
Out of pity, to take what he has just to take.

Suddenly, however, he remembers the quest —
The days of solitude, when everywhere,
It seemed, others were happy on the earth.
Old in his heart, grown pale as the desert,
He looks for the Rose. He sees her in the arms
Of young men, and she is shedding tears for him.

TOWARDS THE WILDERNESS

Trekking the desert the man feels
The atmosphere on him like a knapsack.
He knows the fix upon him of eyes
Hung from huge wings frayed at the edges
Floating dead and black in the sky.

And the Dead Sea, that will neither
Renew nor drown him, a glow rubbed
On the sand, shimmers under the range
In which Nebo can be picked out
As the historic, tall, and bleak one.

He puts the bead of his will on the peak
And does not waver. He is dying:
His plan is to look over the far side
Of the hill on which Moses died looking this way,
And to see the bitter land, and to die of desire.

PART III

THE SCHOOLHOUSE

1

I find it now, the schoolhouse by the tree,
And through the broken door, in the brown light,
I see the benches in rows, the floor he
Paced across, the windows where the fruit
Took the shapes of hearts, and the leaves windled
In the fall, and winter snowed on his head.

In this wreck of a house we were taught
Everything we believed a man could know,
All action, all passion, all ancient thought,
What Socrates had got from Diotima,
How Troilus laughed, in tears, in paradise,
That crowns leapfrog through blood: casts of the dice.

The door hangs from its hinge. Maybe the last
Schoolboy simply forgot to lift the latch
When he rushed out that spring, in his great haste —
Or maybe another, now fat and rich,
Snow-haired in his turn, and plagued by thought,
Burglared back in, looking for the dead light.

2

A man of letters asked the local tramps
To tea. No one came, and he read from Otway
And Chatterton to the walls, and lived for months
On tea. They padlocked the gate when he died.

Snow, sleet, rain, the piss of tramps; and one year
The lock snapped, the gate crowed like a rooster.

And now when the tramps wake sheeted in frost,
They know it is time, they come here and sprawl
At the foot of the statue of their host
Which they call "His Better Self," which he had called
"Knowledge," sometimes "Death," whose one gesture
Seems to beckon and yet remains obscure,

And boil their tea on the floor and pick fruit
In the garden where that man used to walk
Thinking of Eden and the fallen state,
And dust an apple as he had a book —
"Hey now Porky, gie's the core," one hollers;
"Wise up," says Pork, "they ain't gonna be a core."

3
I hear modern schoolchildren shine their pants
In buttock-blessing seats in steamy schools
Soaking up civics and vacant events
From innocents who sponge periodicals
And squeeze that out again in chalky gray
Across the blackboards of the modern day;

Yet they can guess why we fled our benches
Afternoons when we ourselves were just nice
Schoolkids too, who peered out through the branches
For one homely share of the centuries
— Fighting in Latin the wars of the Greeks —
Our green days, the apple we picked and picked

And that was never ours; though they would
Rake their skulls if they found out we returned
By free choice to this house of the dead,
And stand here wondering what that man had learned,

His eyes great pupils and his fishhook teeth
Sunk in the apple of knowledge or death.

4

I recall a recitation in that house:
"*We are the school of Hellas* was the claim.
Maybe it was so. Anyway Hellas
Thought it wasn't, and put the school to flame.
They came back, though, and sifted the ruin."
I think the first inkling of the lesson

Was when we watched him from the apple wrest
Something that put the notion in his brain
The earth was coming to its beautifulest
And would be just like paradise again
The day he died from it. The flames went out
In the blue mantles; he waved us to the night —

And we are here, under the starlight. I
Remember he taught us the stars disperse
In wild flight, though constellated to the eye.
And now I can see the night in its course,
The slow sky uncoiling in exploding forms,
The stars that flee it riding free in its arms.

SEVEN STREAMS OF NEVIS

I

Jack the Blindman, whose violin
Down the harsh weathers of the street
Lifted a scraping bright and sweet,
Joked the sad bars of every tune;
Hardly a dime ever drops there
And he cups *faith* in the clankless air.

Connelly, one-eyed, half blind,
Finding the world blind, in full view
Like wind blew ropes and fences through.
Ticketless at the stiles of the mind
We ask his hope: down, and out,
To swear, "If scum swims to the top of the 'kraut . . ."

They didn't sign up at the desk
Or queue at the bed, though they clapped
The night you bumped and shook and slapped
And ground for free your smart burlesque,
Peaches. We call it mercy when
You give and get nothing and give again.

Tossing in dreams young David Boyle
Could not evade the call of the Lord
For the meek life. He woke and poured
Over his heart the scalding oil
Of *temperance*. Now in his sleep
He yells aloud to God to let him sleep.

Justice made James Lynch Fitzstephen
Hang from a tree his guilty son;
Whereon his heart, twice guilty then,
Hanged itself in his skeleton.
Even Cicero would have known
The unjust who are just are just mad bone.

Natasha, who billowed like silk
On a pole of fire, and weeping went
To one who scrapes the burning tent
While he puffs Luckies and sips milk,
And came home like an empty cage
To find home yet emptier, tried courage.

Sir Henry, seeing that the dew
Gets burned each morning into mist,
Decided fire brings out the best
In things, and that anyone who
Has cooked his eyes at the sunrise
Of beauty, and thumbed himself blind, is wise.

O Connelly! O Jack! O Peaches!
When you fall down foaming in fits
Remember with your scrawny wits
And knee up laughing like leeches:
You are just flesh but you will be
— One rainy day — faith, hope, and charity.

Henry, Natasha, Jimmy, Boyle,
Wrapping your bones the holy flax
Either straitjackets your backs
Or else bags and looks like hell:
Someday the burlap of your skin
Will pass for linen, by the grace of sin.

2

In darkness I climbed Ben Nevis, far from
Your lives. But the seven streams I came on
Were well foreknown.   One sang like strings, one crashed
Through gated rocks, one vibrated, others
Went skipping like unbucketed grease across
Hot stones, or clattered like bones, or like milk
Spilled and billowed in streamers of bright silk,
Irises glimmering a visionary course —
Me grimping the dark, sniffing for the source;
And there I found it windless, lying still,
Dark, high-nested in the mountain, a pool
Whose shined waters on the blackened mountain
Mirrored the black skies; and I rode out on
Dark water under the darkness of the skies,
And the waves ringing through the dark were the rings
Around the eye itself of the world, which,
Drawing down heaven like its black lid, was there
Where merely to be still was temperate,
Where to move was brave, where justice was a glide,
Knowledge the dissolving of the head-hung eyes;
And there my faith lay burning, there my hope
Lay burning on the water, there charity
Burned like a sun.   Oh give, O pool of heaven,
The locus of grace to seven who are whirled
Down the eddies and gutters of the world;
And Connelly and Jack and Peaches, Dave,
Lynch, Natalie, and Hank — seven who have
Bit on your hearts, and spat the gravels of
Tooth and heart, and bit again; who have wiped
The thumb-burst jellies of sight on a sleeve
(The visions we could have wrung from that cloth)
And sprouted sight like mushrooms — O seven
Streams of nothing backgazing after heaven,
In the heart's hell you have it; call it God's Love.

THE DESCENT

for Pierre and Anne-Marie Saville

I

Nailed by our axes to the snow
We belayed. One by one we climbed.
Had somebody in the valley
Been looking up, it must have seemed
A lunatic earthworm headed for paradise,
Or else, if he happened to rub his eyes

While we unroped, and to look back
When we had scattered in the race
Towards dawn, an ascension of crows.
I took the crest as the day broke,
Sure I was first. But Jan must have leapt
The crevasse for a shortcut: he lay there,

Blue lips apart, on the blue snow,
Sprawled on the shellbursts of his heart.
"It's time it went," he gasped. Four years
He had fought in the guerilla wars.
Then he whispered, "Look — the sunrise!"
The same color and nearly the same size,

But behind his back, the new sun
Was rising. When the moon he was
Staring at set in the mountains
He died. On the way down the ice
Had turned so perilous under the sun
There was no choice: we watched while he went down.

2

In Seekonk Woods, on Indian Hill,
It used to seem the branches made
A small green sky that gave off shade.
Once while I lay buried like a quail
In the grass and shadows, a shotgun
Banged, leaves burst, I blinked into the sunshine —

Two crows blown out from either hand
Went clattering away; a third
Swam through the branches to the ground.
I scooped it up, splashed the ford,
And lit out — I must have run half a day
Before I reached Holy Spring. (Anyway,

I thought it was holy. No one
Had told me heaven is overhead.
I only knew people look down
When they pray.) I held the dying bird
As though, should its heartbeat falter,
There wouldn't be much heartbeat anywhere.

After a while I touched the plumes
To the water. In the desert
By the tracks I dug a headstart
Taller than myself. I told him,
"Have a good journey, crow. It can't be far.
It'll be way this side of China, for sure."

3

And had I faced Jan to the sun
Might not the sun have held him here?
Or did he know the day came on
Behind, not glancing back for fear

The moon already was dragging from his bones
The blood as dear to them, and as alien,

As the suit of clothes to a scarecrow
Or the flesh to a cross? Down snow,
Following streambeds through the trees,
We sledded him. To his valleys
Rivers have washed this climber to the sun
The full moon pestled into earth again.

Heaven is in light, overhead,
I have it by heart. Yet the dead
Silting the darkness do not ask
For burials elsewhere than the dusk.
They lie where nothing but the moon can rise,
And make no claims, though they had promises.

Milkweed that grow beside the tombs
Climb from the dead as if in flight,
But a foot high they stop and bloom
In drab shapes, that neither give light
Nor bring up the true darkness of the dead;
Strange, homing lamps, that go out seed by seed.

4

I looked for Indian Hill at Easter.
It was bulldozed. A TV cross
Gleamed from the rooftop of a house
Like sticks of a scarecrow. Once more
I turned and ran for spring: I stumbled on
Fields lying dark and savage and the sun

Reaping its own fire from the trees,
Whirling the faint panic of birds
Up turbulent light. Two white-haired
Crows cried under the wheeling rays;

And loosed as by a scythe, into the sky
A flight of jackdaws rose, earth-birds suddenly

Seized by some thaumaturgic thirst,
Shrill wings flung up the crow-clawed, burned,
Unappeasable air. And one turned,
Dodged through the flock again and burst
Eastward alone, sinking across the wood
On the world-curve of its wings. Nor do we know why,

Mirrored in duskfloods, the fisherbird
Seems to stand in a desolate sky
Feeding at its own heart. In the cry
Eloi! Eloi! flesh was made word:
We hear it in wind catching in the trees,
In lost blood breaking a night through the bones.

WHERE THE TRACK VANISHES

1

The snow revives in the apple trees;
The winter sun seeps from jonquils
Bright as goldmills on the slopes;
Le chemin montant dans les hautes herbes
Curves for the Alps and vanishes.

2

Pierre le Boiteux
— Yellow teeth
Gnashed into gum-level
Stumps, yellow
Eyes beaconing about,
A blackhead the size
Of a huckleberry
Making a cheek sag,
A leg gypsies
Cut the tendon of
So he could beg as a child
Pumping under him,
Twelve goats at heel —
Mounts the track,
Limping through the wild
Grasses — toward where?

3

The track vanishes in a heap of stones
Mortared with weeds and wildflowers —

The fallen church. Nearby stand stones
Of the parish graves, dates worn away,
A handful of carved words visible:
Jacques et Geneviève, priez pour eux —
Véronique DuPrès, regrets éternels —
Sown here even to their fingertips.

Who was it wore the track through the grass?
Surely their mourners are dead, and theirs, and theirs.
Perhaps Pierre limps up every day
Training the goats where to come when it is time,
Foreseeing a terrible loneliness.
No one is lonely here: take Véronique — Jacques,
Husband of another, indifferently dissolves into her.
A skull or two, a couple of pelvises or knees.

4

My hand on the sky
Cannot shut the sky out
Any more than any March
Branch can. In the Boston Store
Once, I tried new shoes:
The shoeman put my feet
In a machine, saying Kid
Wrig yer toes. I
Wrigged and peered:
Inside green shoes green
Twigs were wrigging by themselves
Green as the grasses
I drew from her
Hair in the springtime
While she laughed, unfoliaged
By sunlight, a little
Spray of bones I loved.

5

From villages lost in the valleys —
Moncharvet, St. Bon, La Jaura —
Thin braids of smoke waver upward
Through the clear air. A few lights
Come on, visible from the untracked snow
On the stairway to the Alps. Venus
Shines from the grave of the sun, like
The white gem churched again in its valley.

Once driving from Morristown at night,
We came over a crest: the Fish-Island
Breached shining under the strung-out stars
Of the Galaxy — a long way from Jacques
And Geneviève and Véronique in the prairie.
We stood there not thinking that for them
This was a strange continent to be dying in,
This island under the continent of the stars —

Job's Coffin and the Scorpion; Jacques
And Geneviève side by side in a field of lights;
Capricorn, Ophiocus; the Serpent embracing
The unhinged knees, St. Bon heaped
Like a molted skin: Le Fourmier the arms
Of Hercules; the Swan sailing toward Planay;
Moncharvet, La Jaura by the singing Lyre,
Véronique rocked on the Balances; Champ Béranger —

Fields into which the limping Herdsman wades
Leading his flock up the trackless night, towards
A writhing of lights. Are they Notre Dame des Neiges
Where men ask their God for the daily bread —
Or the March-climbing Virgin carrying wheat?
Where the track vanishes the first land begins.
It goes out everywhere obliterating the horizons.
We must have been walking through it all our lives.

FREEDOM, NEW HAMPSHIRE

I

We came to visit the cow
Dying of fever,
Towle said it was already
Shovelled under, in a secret
Burial-place in the woods.
We prowled through the woods
Weeks, we never

Found where. Other
Kids other summers
Must have found the place
And asked, Why is it
Green here? The rich
Guess a grave, maybe,
The poor think a pit

For dung, like the one
We shovelled in in the fall
That came up green
The next year, that may as well
Have been the grave
Of a cow or something
For all that shows. A kid guesses
By whether his house has a bathroom.

2

We found a cowskull once; we thought it was
From one of the asses in the Bible, for the sun

Shone into the holes through which it had seen
Earth as an endless belt carrying gravel, had heard
Its truculence cursed, had learned how sweat
Stinks, and had brayed — shone into the holes
With solemn and majestic light, as if some
Skull somewhere could be Baalbek or the Parthenon.

That night passing Towle's Barn
We saw lights. Towle had lassoed a calf
By its hind legs, and he tugged against the grip
Of the darkness. The cow stood by chewing millet.
Derry and I took hold, too, and hauled.
It was sopping with darkness when it came free.
It was a bullcalf. The cow mopped it awhile,
And we walked around it with a lantern,

And it was sunburned, somehow, and beautiful.
It took a dug as the first business
And sneezed and drank at the milk of light.
When we got it balanced on its legs, it went wobbling
Towards the night. Walking home in darkness
We saw the July moon looking on Freedom New Hampshire,
We smelled the fall in the air, it was the summer,
We thought, Oh this is but the summer!

3

Once I saw the moon
Drift into the sky like a bright
Pregnancy pared
From a goddess who thought
To be beautiful she must keep slender —
Cut loose, and drifting up there
To happen by itself —
And waning, in lost labor;

As we lost our labor
Too — afternoons
When we sat on the gate

By the pasture, under the Ledge,
Buzzing and skirling on toilet-
papered combs tunes
To the rumble-seated cars
Taking the Ossipee Road

On Sundays; for
Though dusk would come upon us
Where we sat, and though we had
Skirled out our hearts in the music,
Yet the dandruffed
Harps we skirled it on
Had done not much better than
Flies, which buzzed, when quick

We trapped them in our hands,
Which went silent when we
Crushed them, which we bore
Downhill to the meadowlark's
Nest full of throats
Which Derry charmed and combed
With an Arabian air, while I
Chucked crushed flies into

Innards I could not see,
For the night had fallen
And the crickets shrilled on all sides
In waves, as if the grassleaves
Shrieked by hillsides
As they grew, and the stars
Made small flashes in the sky,
Like mica flashing in rocks

On the chokecherried Ledge
Where bees I stepped on once
Hit us from behind like a shotgun,
And where we could see
Windowpanes in Freedom flash

And Loon Lake and Winnipesaukee
Flash in the sun
And the blue world flashing.

4

The fingerprints of our eyeballs would zigzag
On the sky; the clouds that came drifting up
Our fingernails would drift into the thin air;
In bed at night there was music if you listened,
Of an old surf breaking far away in the blood.

Kids who come by chance on grass green for a man
Can guess cow, dung, man, anything they want,
To them it is the same. To us who knew him as he was
After the beginning and before the end, it is green
For a name called out of the confusions of the earth —

Winnipesaukee coined like a moon, a bullcalf
Dragged from the darkness where it breaks up again,
Larks which long since have crashed for good in the grass
To which we fed the flies, buzzing ourselves like flies,
While the crickets shrilled beyond us, in July. . .

The mind may sort it out and give it names —
When a man dies he dies trying to say without slurring
The abruptly decaying sounds. It is true
That only flesh dies, and spirit flowers without stop
For men, cows, dung, for all dead things; and it is good, yes —

But an incarnation is in particular flesh
And the dust that is swirled into a shape
And crumbles and is swirled again had but one shape
That was this man. When he is dead the grass
Heals what he suffered, but he remains dead,
And the few who loved him know this until they die.

For my brother, 1925–1957

THE SUPPER AFTER THE LAST

for Anne Buchanan

1

The desert moves out on half the horizon
Rimming the illusory water which, among islands,
Bears up the sky. The sea scumbles in
From its own inviolate border under the sky.
A dragon-fly floating on six legs on the sand
Lifts its green-yellow tail, declines its wings
A little, flutters them a little, and lays
On dazzled sand the shadow of its wings. Near shore
A bather wades through his shadow in the water.
He tramples and kicks it; it recomposes.

2

Outside the open door
Of the whitewashed house,
Framed in its doorway, a chair,
Vacant, waits in the sunshine.

A jug of fresh water stands
Inside the door. In the sunshine
The chair waits, less and less vacant.
The host's plan is to offer water, then stand aside.

3

They eat rosé and chicken. The chicken head
Has been tucked under the shelter of the wing.

Under the table a red-backed, passionate dog
Cracks chicken bones on the blood and gravel floor.

No one else but the dog and the blind
Cat watching it knows who is that bearded
Wild man guzzling overhead, the wreck of passion
Emptying his eyes, who has not yet smiled,

Who stares at the company, where he is company,
Turns them to sacks of appalled, grinning skin,
Forks the fowl-eye out from under
The large, makeshift, cooked lid, evaporates the wine,

Jellies the sunlit table and spoons, floats
The deluxe grub down the intestines of the Styx,
Devours all but the cat and the dog, to whom he slips scraps,
The red-backed accomplice busy grinding gristle.

4

When the bones of the host
Crack in the hound's jaw
The wild man rises. Opening
His palms he announces:
I came not to astonish
But to destroy you. Your
Jug of cool water? Your
Hanker after wings? Your
Lech for transcendence?
I came to prove you are
Intricate and simple things
As you are, created
In the image of nothing,
Taught of the creator
By your images in dirt —
As mine, for which you set
A chair in the sunshine,

Mocking me with water!
As pictures of wings,
Not even iridescent,
That clasp the sand
And that cannot perish, you swear,
Having once been evoked!

5

The witnesses back off; the scene begins to float in water;
Far out in that mirage the Saviour sits whispering to the world,
Becoming a mirage. The dog turns into a smear on the sand.
The cat grows taller and taller as it flees into space.

From the hot shine where he sits his whispering drifts:
You struggle from flesh into wings; the change exists.
But the wings that live gripping the contours of the dirt
Are all at once nothing, flesh and light lifted away.

You are the flesh; I am the resurrection, because I am the light.
I cut to your measure the creeping piece of darkness
That haunts you in the dirt. Steps into light —
I make you over. I breed the shape of your grave in the dirt.

PART IV

THE AVENUE BEARING THE INITIAL OF CHRIST INTO THE NEW WORLD

Was diese kleine Gasse doch für ein Reich an sich war . . .

for Gail

I

pcheek pcheek pcheek pcheek pcheek
They cry. The motherbirds thieve the air
To appease them. A tug on the East River
Blasts the bass-note of its passage, lifted
From the infra-bass of the sea. A broom
Swishes over the sidewalk like feet through leaves.
Valerio's pushcart Ice Coal Kerosene
Moves   clack
                    clack
                                clack
On a broken wheelrim. Ringing in its chains
The New Star Laundry horse comes down the street
Like a roofleak whucking in a pail.
At the redlight, where a horn blares,
The Golden Harvest Bakery brakes on its gears,
Squeaks, and seethes in place. A propane-
gassed bus makes its way with big, airy sighs.

Across the street a woman throws open
Her window,
She sets, terribly softly,
Two potted plants on the windowledge
              tic   tic
And bangs shut her window.

A man leaves a doorway tic toc tic toc tic toc tic hurrah
    toc splat on Avenue C tic etc and turns the corner.

Banking the same corner
A pigeon coasts 5th Street in shadows,
Looks for altitude, surmounts the rims of buildings,
And turns white.

The babybirds pipe down. It is day.

2

In sunlight on the Avenue
The Jew rocks along in a black fur shtraimel,
Black robe, black knickers, black knee-stockings,
Black shoes. His beard like a sod-bottom
Hides the place where he wears no tie.
A dozen children troop after him, barbels flying,
In skullcaps. They are Reuben, Simeon, Levi, Judah, Issachar,
    Zebulun, Benjamin, Dan, Naphtali, Gad, Asher.
With the help of the Lord they will one day become
Courtiers, thugs, rulers, rabbis, asses, adders, wrestlers,
    bakers, poets, cartpushers, infantrymen.

The old man is sad-faced. He is near burial
And one son is missing. The women who bore him sons
And are past bearing, mourn for the son
And for the father, wondering if the man will go down
Into the grave of a son mourning, or if at the last
The son will put his hands on the eyes of his father.

The old man wades towards his last hour.
On 5th Street, between Avenues A and B,
In sunshine, in his private cloud, Bunko Certified Embalmer,
Cigar in his mouth, nose to the wind, leans
At the doorway of Bunko's Funeral Home & Parlour,
Glancing west towards the Ukrainians, eastward idly
Where the Jew rocks towards his last hour.

Sons, grandsons at his heel, the old man
Confronts the sun. He does not feel its rays
Through his beard, he does not understand
Fruits and vegetables live by the sun.
Like his children he is sallow-faced, he sees
A blinding signal in the sky, he smiles.

Bury me not Bunko damned Catholic I pray you in Egypt.

3

From the Station House
Under demolishment on Houston
To the Power Station on 14th,
Jews, Negroes, Puerto Ricans
Walk in the spring sunlight.

The Downtown Talmud Torah
Blosztein's Cutrate Bakery
Areceba Panataria Hispano
Peanuts Dried Fruit Nuts & Canned Goods
Productos Tropicales
Appetizing Herring Candies Nuts
Nathan Kugler Chicken Store Fresh Killed Daily
Little Rose Restaurant
Rubinstein the Hatter Mens Boys Hats Caps Furnishings
J. Herrmann Dealer in All Kinds of Bottles
Natural Bloom Cigars
Blony Bubblegum
Mueren las Cucarachas Super Potente Garantizada de Matar las
        Cucarachas mas Resistentes
Wenig מצבות
G. Schnee Stairbuilder
Everyouth la Original Loción Eterna Juventud Satisfacción Dinero
        Devuelto
Happy Days Bar & Grill

Through dust-stained windows over storefronts
Curtains drawn aside, onto the Avenue

69

Thronged with Puerto Ricans, Negroes, Jews,
Baby carriages stuffed with groceries and babies,
The old women peer, blessed damozels
Sitting up there young forever in the cockroached rooms,
Eating fresh-killed chicken, productos tropicales,
Appetizing herring, canned goods, nuts;
They puff out smoke from Natural Bloom cigars
And one day they puff like Blony Bubblegum.
Across the square skies with faces in them
Pigeons skid, crashing into the brick.
From a rooftop a boy fishes at the sky,
Around him a flock of pigeons fountains,
Blown down and swirling up again, seeking the sky.
From a skyview of the city they must seem
A whirlwind on the desert seeking itself;
Here they break from the rims of the buildings
Without rank in the blue military cemetery sky.
A red kite wriggles like a tadpole
Into the sky beyond them, crosses
The sun, lays bare its own crossed skeleton.

To fly from this place — to roll
On some bubbly blacktop in the summer,
To run under the rain of pigeon plumes, to be
Tarred, and feathered with birdshit, Icarus,

In Kugler's glass headdown dangling by yellow legs.

4

First Sun Day of the year. Tonight,
When the sun will have turned from the earth,
She will appear outside Hy's Luncheonette,
The crone who sells the News and the Mirror,
The oldest living thing on Avenue C,
Outdating much of its brick and mortar.
If you ask for the News she gives you the Mirror
And squints long at the nickel in her hand
Despising it, perhaps, for being a nickel,

And stuffs it in her apron pocket
And sucks her lips. Rain or stars, every night
She is there, squatting on the orange crate,
Issuing out only in darkness, like the cucarachas
And strange nightmares in the chambers overhead.
She can't tell one newspaper from another,
She has forgotten how Nain her dead husband looked,
She has forgotten her children's whereabouts
Or how many there were, or what the *News*
And *Mirror* tell about that we buy them with nickels.
She is sure only of the look of a nickel
And that there is a Lord in the sky overhead.
She dwells in a flesh that is of the Lord
And drifts out, therefore, only in darkness
Like the streetlamp outside the Luncheonette
Or the lights in the secret chamber
In the firmament, where Yahweh himself dwells.
Like Magdelene in the Battistero of Saint John
On the carved-up continent, in the land of sun,
She lives shadowed, under a feeble bulb
That lights her face, her crab's hands, her small bulk on the crate.

She is Pulchería mother of murderers and madmen,
She is also Alyona whose neck was a chicken leg.

Mother was it the insufferable wind?
She sucks her lips a little further into the mousehole.
She stares among the stars, and among the streetlamps.

The mystery is hers.

5

That violent song of the twilight!
Now, in the silence, will the motherbirds
Be dead, and the infantbirds
That were in the dawn merely transparent
Unfinished things, nothing but bellies,

Will they have been shoved out
And in the course of a morning, casually,
On scrawny wings, have taken up the life?

6

In the pushcart market, on Sunday,
A crate of lemons discharges light like a battery.
Icicle-shaped carrots that through black soil
Wove away lie like flames in the sun.
Onions with their shirts ripped seek sunlight
On green skins. The sun beats
On beets dirty as boulders in cowfields,
On turnips pinched and gibbous
From budging rocks, on embery sweets,
Peanut-shaped Idahos, shore-pebble Long Islands and Maines,
On horseradishes still growing weeds on the flat ends,
Cabbages lying about like sea-green brains
The skulls have been shucked from,
On tomatoes, undented plum-tomatoes, alligator-skinned
Cucumbers, that float pickled
In the wooden tubs of green skim milk —

Sky-flowers, dirt-flowers, underdirt-flowers,
Those that climbed for the sun in their lives
And those that wormed away — equally uprooted,
Maimed, lopped, shucked, and misaimed.

In the market in Damascus a goat
Came to a stall where twelve goatheads
Were lined up for sale. It sniffed them
One by one. Finally thirteen goats started
Smiling in their faintly sardonic way.

A crone buys a pickle from a crone,
It is wrapped in the *Mirror*,
At home she will open the wrapping, stained,
And stare and stare and stare at it.

And the cucumbers, and the melons,
And the leeks, and the onions, and the garlic.

7

Already the Avenue troughs the light of day.
Southwards, towards Houston and Pitt,
Where Avenue C begins, the eastern ranges
Of the wiped-out lives — punks, lushes,
Panhandlers, pushers, rumsoaks, everyone
Who took it easy when he should have been out failing at some-
        thing —
The pots-and-pans man pushes his cart,
Through the intersection of the light, at 3rd,
Where sunset smashes on the aluminum of it,
On the bottoms, curves, handles, metal panes,
Mirrors: of the bead-curtained cave under the falls
In Freedom, Seekonk Woods leafing the light out,
Halfway to Kingston where a road branched out suddenly,
Between Pamplonne and Les Salins two meeting paths
Over a sea the green of churchsteeple copper.
Of all places on earth inhabited by men
Why is it we find ourselves on this Avenue
Where the dusk gets worse,
And the mirrorman pushing his heaped mirrors
Into the shadows between 3rd and 2nd,
Pushes away a mess of old pots and pans?

The ancient Negro sits as usual
Outside the Happy Days Bar & Grill. He wears
Dark glasses. Every once in a while, abruptly,
He starts to sing, chanting in a hoarse, nearly breaking
Voice —

oooooooooooooo v   jawwwwwww
            u h   w w
              u h   w w
                              w din

73

And becomes silent
     Stares into the polaroid Wilderness
Gross-Rosen, Maidanek, Flössenberg, Ravensbruck, Stutthof, Riga,
Bergen-Belsen, Mauthausen, Birkenau, Treblinka, Natzweiler,
Dachau, Buchenwald, Auschwitz —
                      Villages,
Pasture-bordered hamlets on the far side of the river.

8

The promise was broken too freely
To them and to their fathers, for them to care.
They survive like cedars on a cliff, roots
Hooked in any crevice they can find.
They walk Avenue C in shadows
Neither conciliating its Baalim
Nor whoring after landscapes of the senses,
Tarig bab el Amoud being in the blood
Fumigated by Puerto Rican cooking.

Among women girthed like cedar trees
Other, slenderer ones appear:
One yellow haired, in August,
Under shooting stars on the lake, who
Believed in promises which broke by themselves —
In a German flower garden in the Bronx
The wedding of a child and a child, one flesh
Divided in the Adirondack spring —
One who found in the desert city of the West
The first happiness, and fled therefore —
And by a southern sea, in the pines, one loved
Until the mist rose blue in the trees
Around the spiderwebs that kept on shining,
Each day of the shortening summer.

And as rubbish burns
And the pushcarts are loaded

With fruit and vegetables and empty crates
And clank away on iron wheels over cobblestones,
And merchants infold their stores
And the carp ride motionlessly sleeplessly
In the dark tank in the fishmarket,
The figures withdraw into chambers overhead —
In the city of the mind, chambers built
Of care and necessity, where, hands lifted to the blinds,
They glimpse in mirrors backed with the blackness of the world
Awkward, cherished rooms containing the familiar selves.

9

Children set fires in ashbarrels,
Cats prowl the fires, scraps of fishes burn.

A child lay in the flames.
It was not the plan. Abraham
Stood in terror at the duplicity.
Isaac whom he loved lay in the flames.
The Lord turned away washing
His hands without soap and water
Like a common housefly.

The children laugh.
Isaac means he *laughs*.
Maybe the last instant,
The dying itself, *is* easier,
Easier anyway than the hike
From Pitt the blind gut
To the East River of Fishes,
Maybe it is as the poet said,
And the soul turns to thee
O vast and well-veiled Death
And the body gratefully nestles close to thee —

I think of Isaac reading Whitman in Chicago,
The week before he died, coming across

Such a passage and muttering, Oi!
What shit! And smiling, but not for you — I mean,

For *thee*, Sane and Sacred Death!

10

It was Gold's junkhouse, the one the clacking
Carts that little men pad after in harnesses
Picking up bedbugged mattresses, springs
The stubbornness has been loved out of,
Chairs felled by fat, lampshades lights have burned through,
Linoleum the geometry has been scuffed from,
Carriages a single woman's work has brought to wreck,
Would come to in the dusk and unload before,
That the whole neighborhood came out to see
Burning in the night, flames opening out like
Eyelashes from the windows, men firing the tears in,
Searchlights coming on like streams of water, smashing
On the brick, the water blooming up the wall
Like pale trees, reaching into the darkness beyond.

Nobody mourned, nobody stood around in pajamas
And a borrowed coat steaming his nose in coffee.
It was only Gold's junkhouse.
                              But this evening
The neighborhood comes out again, everything
That may abide the fire was made to go through the fire
And it was made clean: a few twisted springs,
Charred mattresses (crawling still, naturally),
Perambulator skeletons, bicycles tied in knots —
In a great black pile at the junkhouse door,
Smelling of burnt rubber and hair. Rustwater
Hangs in icicles over the windows and door,
Like frozen piss aimed at trespassers,
Combed by wind, set overnight. Carriages we were babies in,
Springs that used to resist love, that gave in

And were thrown out like whores — the black
Irreducible heap, mausoleum of what we were —
It is cold suddenly, we feel chilled,
Nobody knows for sure what is left of him.

11

The fishmarket closed, the fishes gone into flesh.
The smelts draped on each other, fat with roe,
The marble cod hacked into chunks on the counter,
Butterfishes mouths still open, still trying to eat,
Porgies with receding jaws hinged apart
In a grimace of dejection, as if like cows
They had died under the sledgehammer, perches
In grass-green armor, spotted squeteagues
In the melting ice meek-faced and croaking no more,
Except in the plip plop plip plip in the bucket,
Mud-eating mullets buried in crushed ice,
Tilefishes with scales like chickenfat,
Spanish mackerels, buttercups on the flanks,
Pot-bellied pikes, two-tone flounders
After the long contortion of pushing both eyes
To the brown side that they might look up,
Brown side down, like a mass laying-on of hands,
Or the oath-taking of an army.

The only things alive are the carp
That drift in the black tank in the rear,
Kept living for the usual reason, that they have not died,
And perhaps because the last meal was garbage and they might
    begin stinking
On dying, before the customer was halfway home.
They nudge each other, to be netted,
The sweet flesh to be lifted thrashing in the air,
To be slugged, and then to keep on living
While they are opened on the counter.

Fishes do not die exactly, it is more
That they go out of themselves, the visible part
Remains the same, there is little pallor,
Only the cataracted eyes which have not shut ever
Must look through the mist which crazed Homer.

These are the vegetables of the deep,
The Sheol-flowers of darkness, swimmers
Of denser darknesses where the sun's rays bend for the last time
And in the sky there burns this shifty jellyfish
That degenerates and flashes and re-forms.

Motes in the eye land is the lid of,
They are plucked out of the green skim milk of the eye.

Fishes are nailed on the wood,
The big Jew stands like Christ, nailing them to the wood,
He scrapes the knife up the grain, the scales fly,
He unnails them, reverses them, nails them again,
Scrapes and the scales fly. He lops off the heads,
Shakes out the guts as if they did not belong in the first place,
And they are flesh for the first time in their lives.

Dear Frau ——————— :

    Your husband, ——————— , died in the Camp Hospital
on ———————. May I express my sincere sympathy on your
bereavement. ——————— was admitted to the Hospital on
——————— with severe symptoms of exhaustion, complaining
of difficulties in breathing and pains in the chest. Despite
competent medication and devoted medical attention, it
proved impossible, unfortunately, to keep the patient alive.
The deceased voiced no final requests.

Camp Commandant, ———————

On 5th Street Bunko Certified Embalmer Catholic
Leans in his doorway drawing on a Natural Bloom Cigar.
He looks up the street. Even the Puerto Ricans are Jews
And the Chinese Laundry closes on Saturday.

12

Next door, outside the pink-fronted Bodega Hispano —

(A crying: you imagine
Some baby in its crib, wailing
As if it could foresee everything.
The crying subsides: you imagine
A mother or father clasping
The damned creature in their arms.
It breaks out again,
This time in a hair-raising shriek — ah,
The alleycat, in a pleasant guise,
In the darkness outside, in the alley,
Wauling, shrieking slowly in its blood.

Another, loftier shrieking
Drowns it out. It begins always
On the high note, over a clang of bells:
Hook & Ladder 11 with an explosion of mufflers
Crab-walking out of 5th Street,
Accelerating up the Avenue, siren
Sliding on the rounded distances
Returning fainter and fainter,
Like a bee looping away from where you lie in the grass.

The searchlights catch him at the topfloor window,
Trying to move, nailed in place by the shine.

The bells of Saint Brigid's
On Tompkins Square
Toll for someone who has died —
J'oïs la cloche de Serbonne,
Qui tousjours à neuf heures sonne
Le Salut que l'Ange prédit . . .

Expecting the visitation
You lie back on your bed,
The sounds outside
Must be outside. Here
Are only the dead spirituals
Turning back into prayers —
You rise on an elbow
To make sure they come from outside,
You hear nothing, you lay down
Your head on the pillow
Like a pick-up arm —
    swing low
          swing low
                    sweet
   lowsweet —)

— Carols of the Caribbean, plinkings of guitars.

13

The garbage disposal truck
Like a huge hunched animal
That sucks in garbage in the place
Where other animals evacuate it
Whines, as the cylinder in the rear
Threshes up the trash and garbage,
Where two men in rubber suits
(It must be raining outside)
Heap it in. The groaning motor

Rises in a whine as it grinds in
The garbage, and between-times
Groans. It whines and groans again.
All about it as it moves down
5th Street is the clatter of trashcans,
The crashes of them as the sanitary engineers
Bounce them on the sidewalk.

If it is raining outside
You can only tell by looking
In puddles, under the lifted streetlamps.

It would be the spring rain.

14

Behind the Power Station on 14th, the held breath
Of light, as God is a held breath, withheld,
Spreads the East River, into which fishes leak:
The brown sink or dissolve,
The white float out in shoals and armadas,
Even the gulls pass them up, pale
Bloated socks of riverwater and rotted seed,
That swirl on the tide, punched back
To the Hell Gate narrows, and on the ebb
Steam seaward, seeding the sea.

On the Avenue, through air tinted crimson
By neon over the bars, the rain is falling.
You stood once on Houston, among panhandlers and winos
Who weave the eastern ranges, learning to be free,
To not care, to be knocked flat and to get up clear-headed
Spitting the curses out. "Now be nice,"
The proprietor threatens; "Be nice," he cajoles.
"Fuck you," the bum shouts as he is hoisted again,
"God fuck your mother." (In the empty doorway,
Hunched on the empty crate, the crone gives no sign.)

That night a wildcat cab whined crosstown on 7th.
You knew even the traffic lights were made by God,
The red splashes growing dimmer the farther away
You looked, and away up at 14th, a few green stars;
And without sequence, and nearly all at once,
The red lights blinked into green,
And just before there was one complete Avenue of green,
The little green stars in the distance blinked.

It is night, and raining. You look down
Towards Houston in the rain, the living streets,
Where instants of transcendence
Drift in oceans of loathing and fear, like lanternfishes,
Or phosphorus flashings in the sea, or the feverish light
Skin is said to give off when the swimmer drowns at night.

From the blind gut Pitt to the East River of Fishes
The Avenue cobbles a swath through the discolored air,
A roadway of refuse from the teeming shores and ghettos
And the Caribbean Paradise, into the new ghetto and new paradise,
This God-forsaken Avenue bearing the initial of Christ
Through the haste and carelessness of the ages,
The sea standing in heaps, which keeps on collapsing,
Where the drowned suffer a C-change,
And remain the common poor.

Since Providence, for the realization of some unknown purpose, has
seen fit to leave this dangerous people on the face of the earth, and
did not destroy it. . .

Listen! the swish of the blood,
The sirens down the bloodpaths of the night,
Bone tapping on the bone, nerve-nets
Singing under the breath of sleep —

We scattered over the lonely seaways,
Over the lonely deserts did we run,
In dark lanes and alleys we did hide ourselves . . .

The lungs put out the light of the world as they
The heart beats without windows in its night,
Heave and collapse, the brain turns and rattles
In its own black axlegrease —

                    In the nighttime
Of the blood they are laughing and saying,
Our little lane, what a kingdom it was!

                  oi weih, oi weih